BOLD K

Clouds

DISCOVER THIS CHILDREN'S EARTH SCIENCE BOOK WITH FACTS!

No part of this book may be reproduced or used in any way or form or by any means whether electronic or mechanical, this means that you cannot record or photocopy any material ideas or tips that are provided in this book.
Copyright 2022

All images in this book have been reproduced with the knowledge and prior consent of the artists concerned, and no responsibility is accepted by producer, publisher, or printer for any infringement of copyright or otherwise, arising from the contents of this publication.

If you'd like your child to learn about the clouds, you should give him or her a Facts about Clouds for Kids book. This fun book contains beautiful pictures and interesting facts about clouds. It will also be useful for school projects.

In addition to its educational value, this book is great for personal use. You can also use it to help you teach about the different types of clouds. This is a great book for kids because it is not only enjoyable but can also help them understand the importance of clouds.

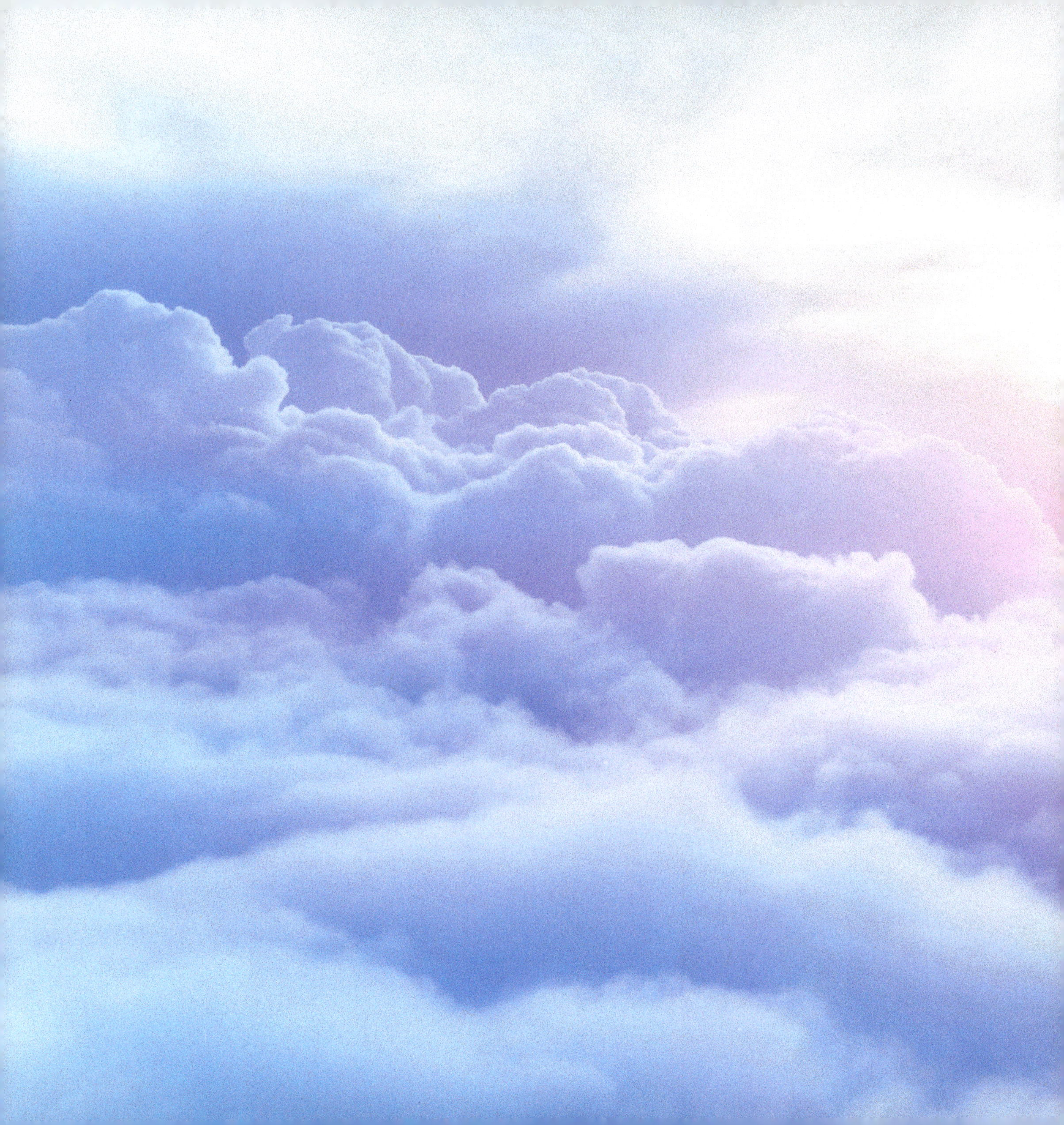

The first thing to teach your child about clouds is that they are formed from very tiny drops of water or ice. These droplets float in the air and appear as if they're floating on water.

It is important to explain this phenomenon to children, so they can identify and recognize different kinds of clouds.
A flashlight can help them understand how tiny these droplets are. This helps them to understand why clouds are so beautiful.

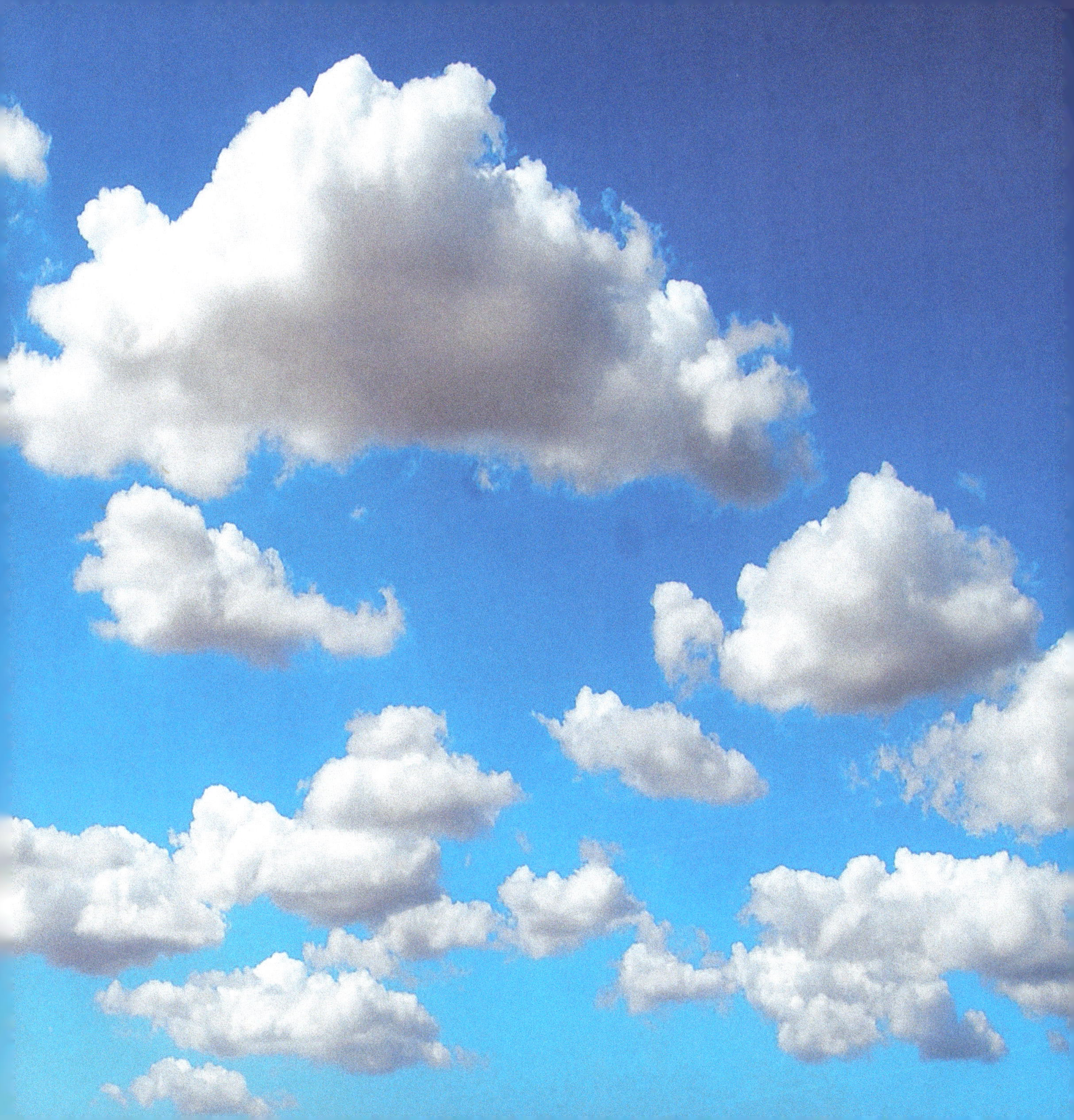

The formation of clouds is very complicated. In order to understand them, you must teach your children how these clouds form. There are several factors that determine how clouds form. One of them is the amount of heat in the ground.

This heat will influence the formation of clouds. When these conditions meet, these droplets will form cloud shapes and forms. When these factors are present in an area with higher moisture, the weather can be quite unpredictable.

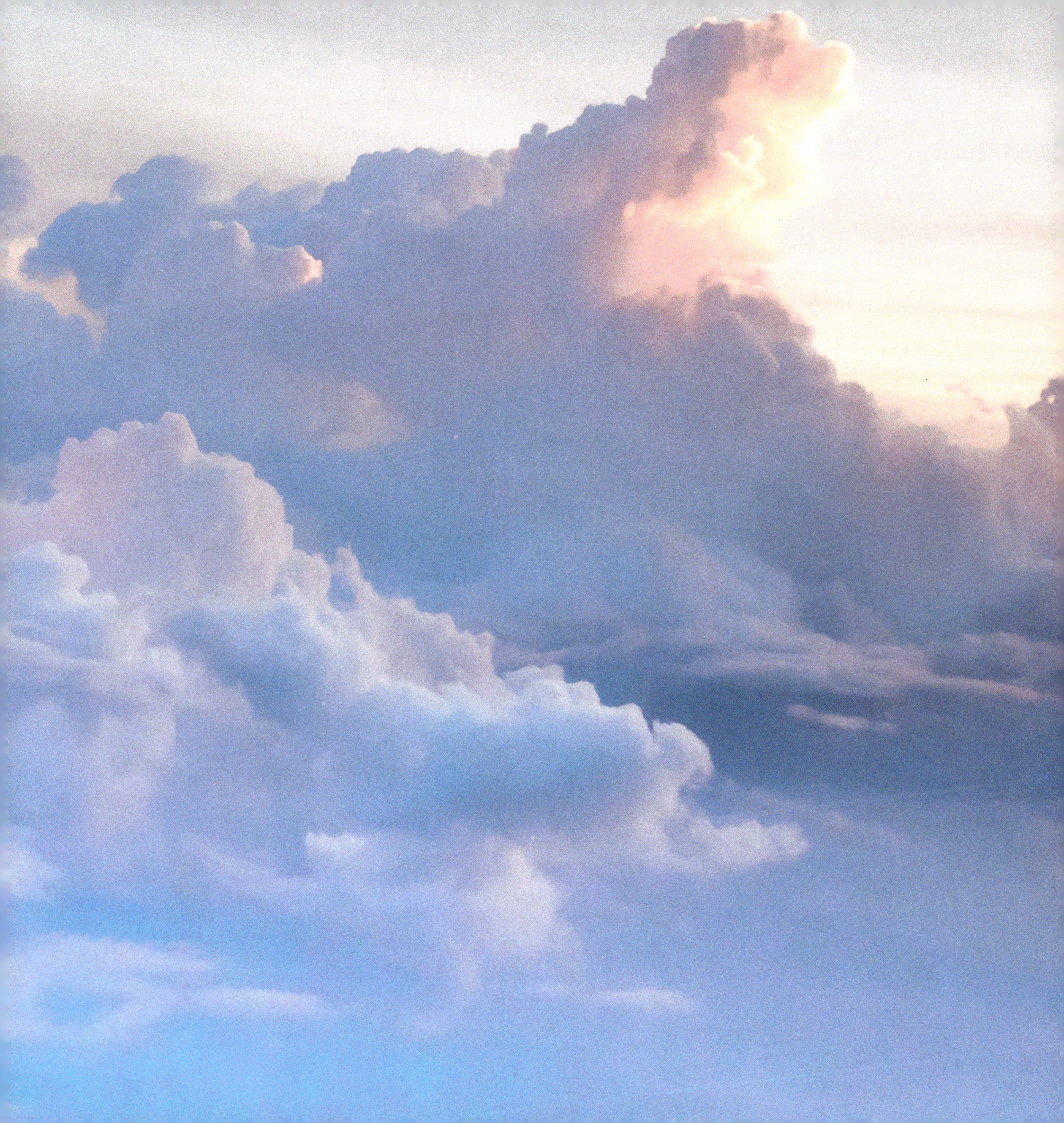

Another interesting fact about clouds for kids is that there are three major types of clouds. Stratus clouds form at high elevations, typically more than 2000 meters above the ground. These clouds are often seen as blankets covering the entire sky, and are more common in mountainous areas.

They also form over hills that rise above valleys. Unlike nimbus clouds, stratus clouds rarely produce rain. Meanwhile, nimbus clouds may produce heavy rain or only a light drizzle.

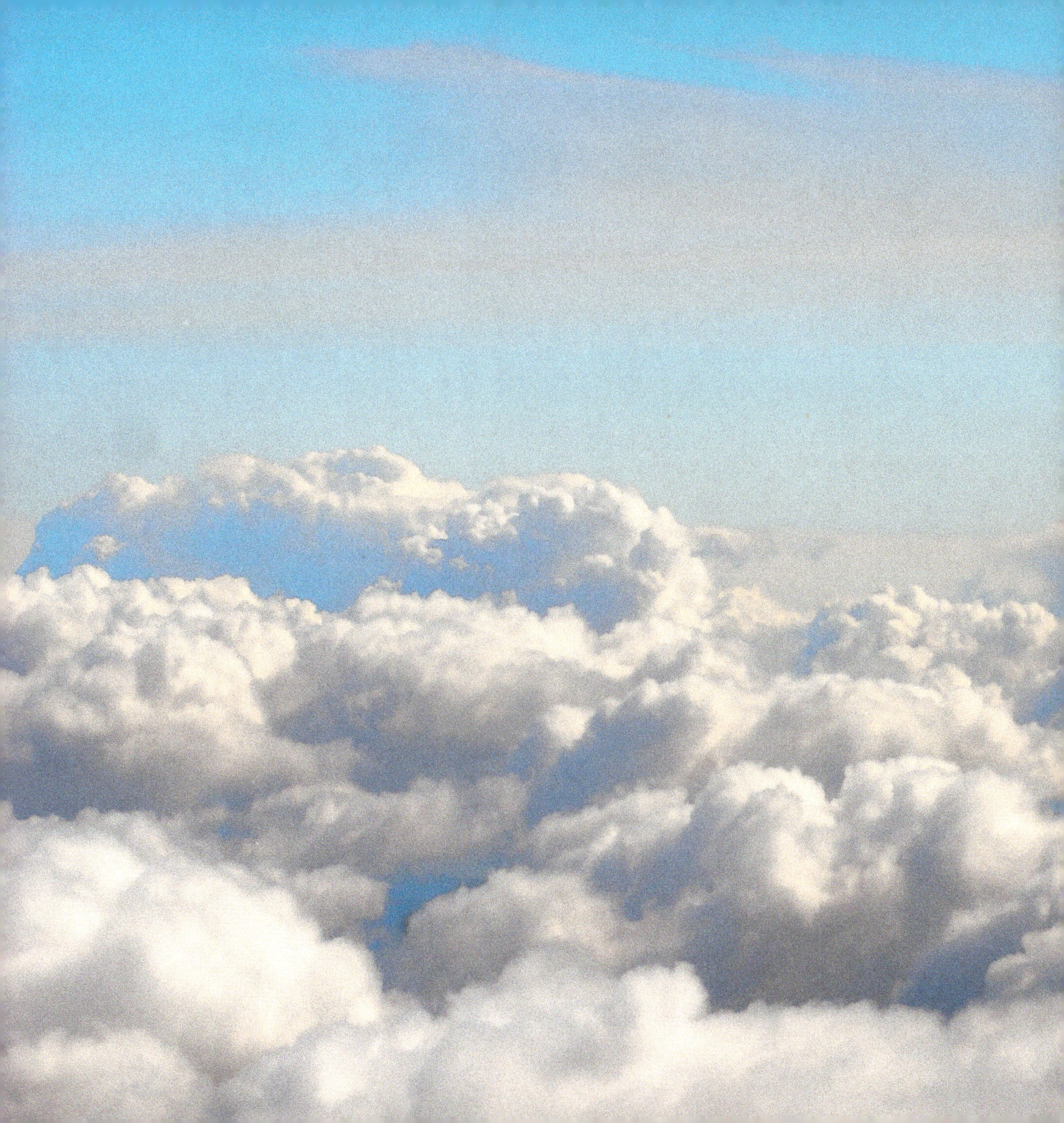

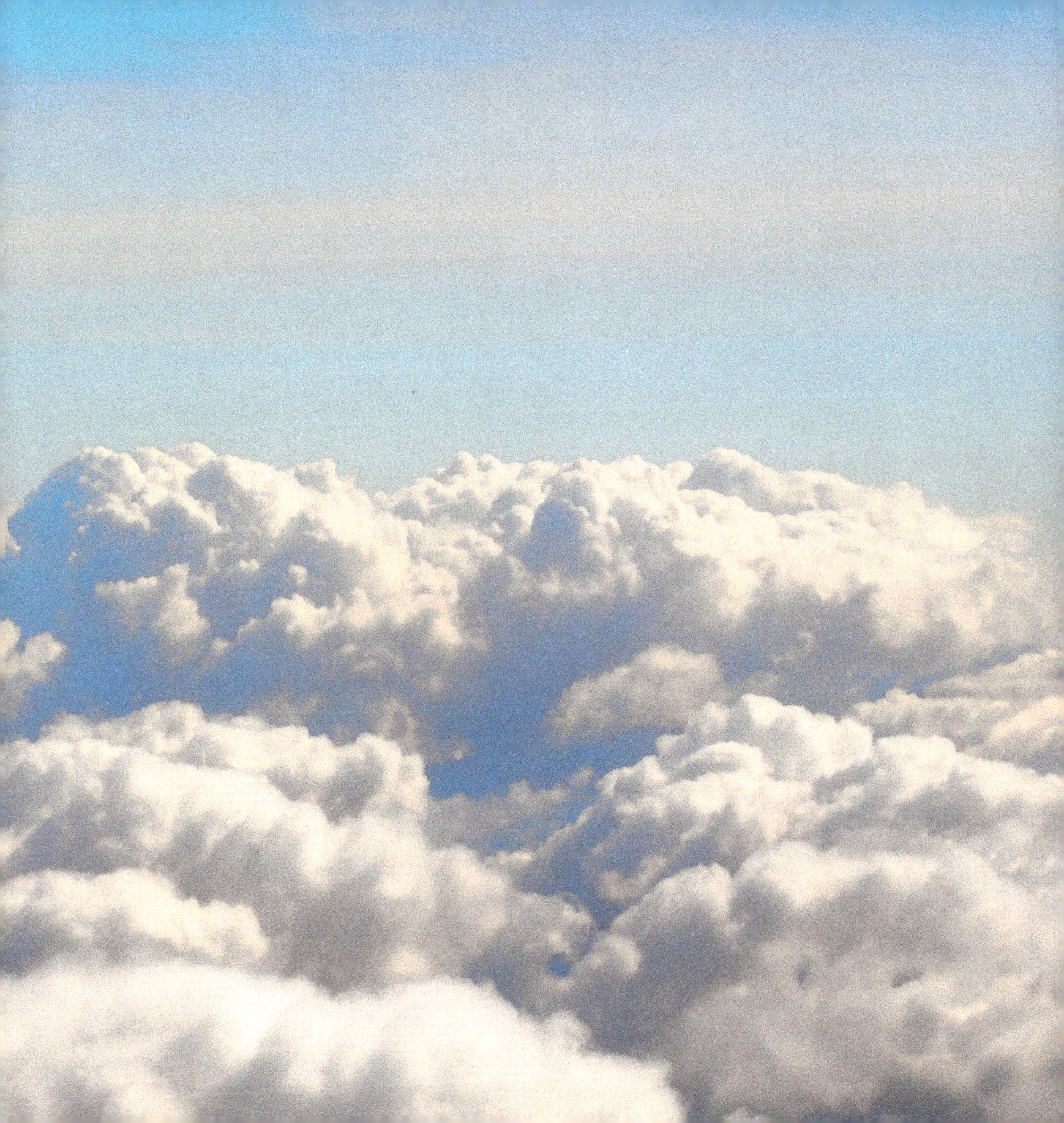

Stratus clouds are found at lower altitudes, and they resemble various objects. Stratus clouds are often seen in mountainous areas, where they form as blankets of clouds that cover the entire sky. However, they are rarely accompanied by rain.

Despite their name, clouds are essentially billowing formations of water and ice in the atmosphere. Besides, they are extremely beautiful. But the clouds in the sky can also be scary.

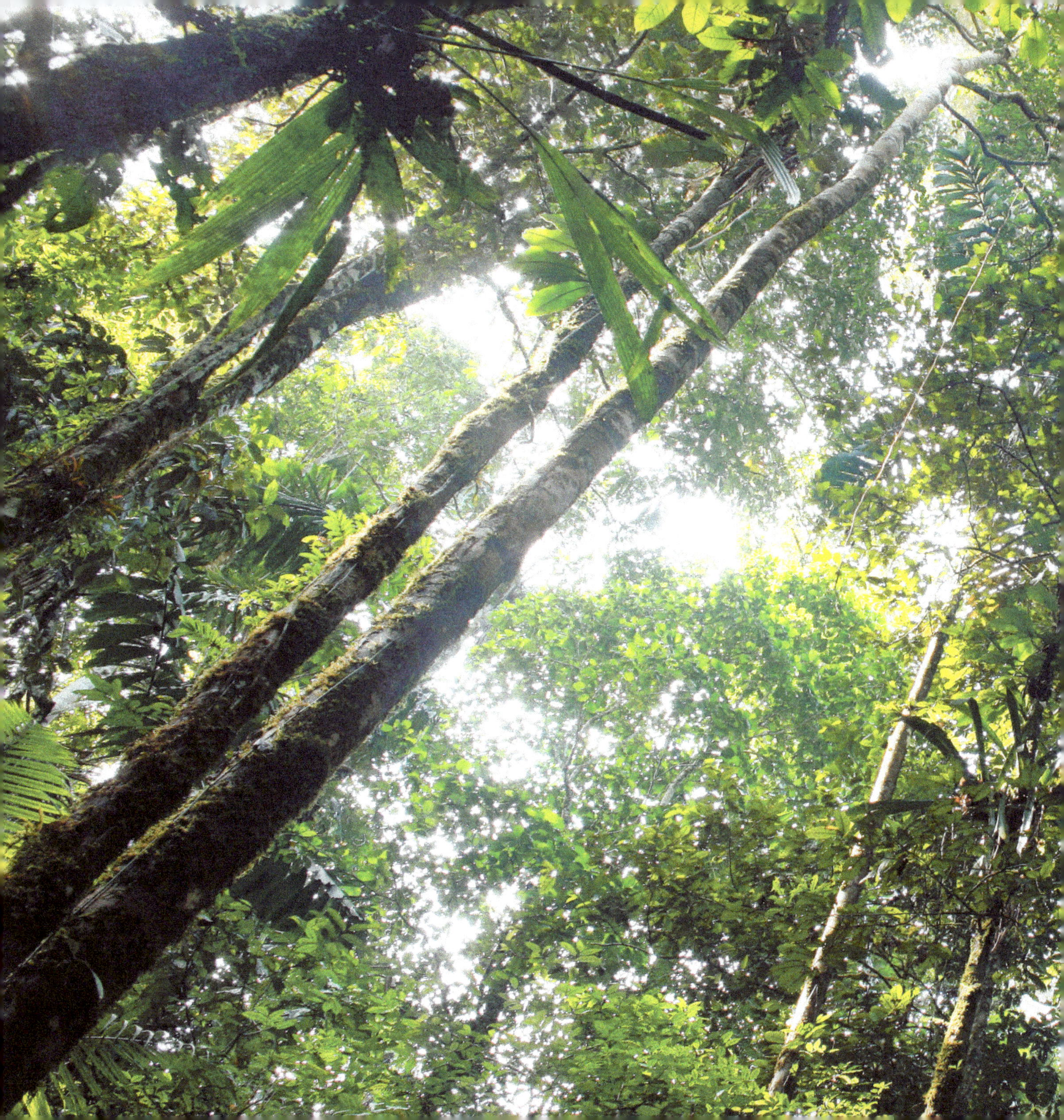

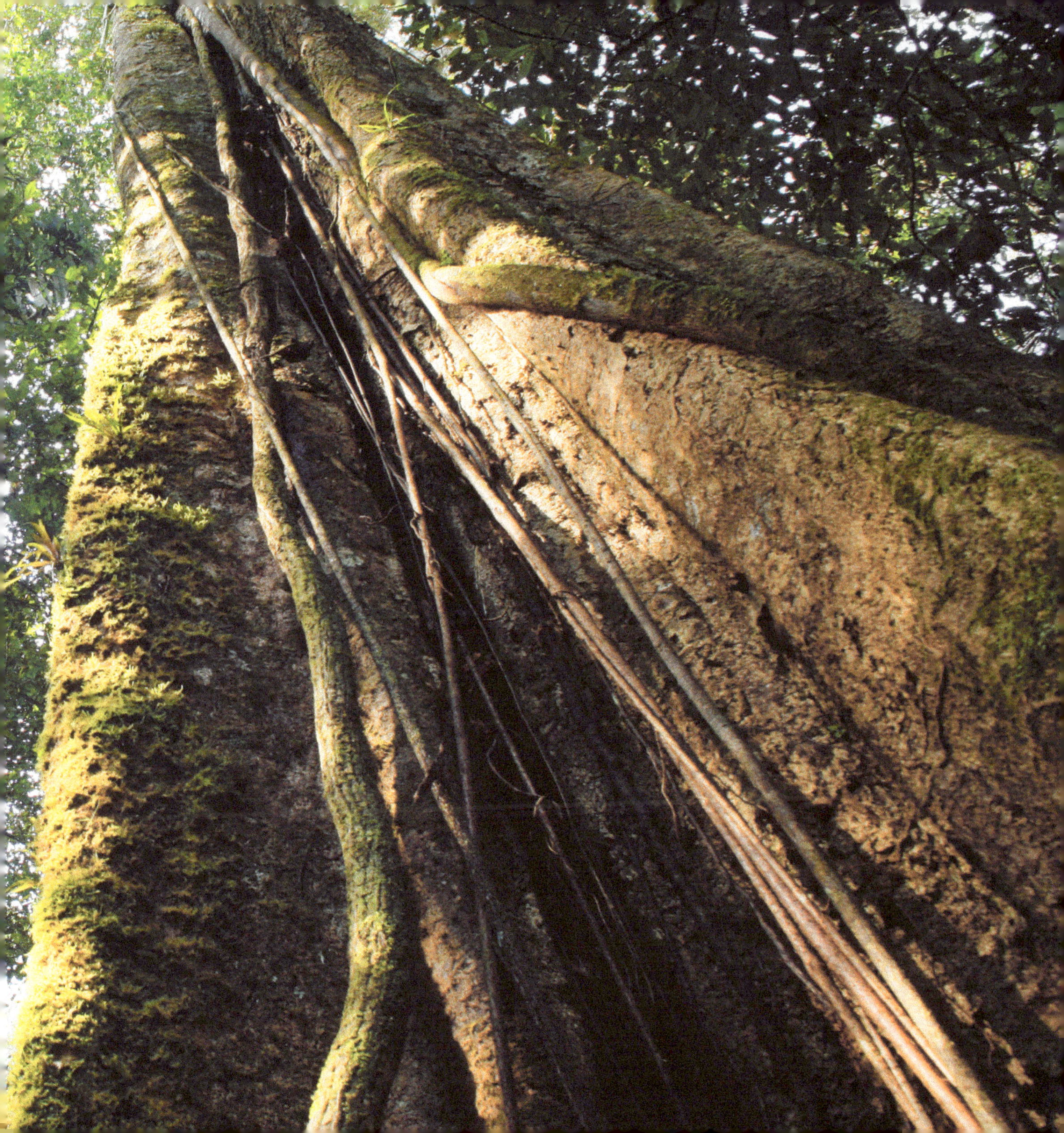

Stratus clouds are the most popular types of clouds. They are cloudy, with a thin layer of water, and appear to float in the air. Stratus clouds are found in mountains and are commonly seen as blankets of clouds that cover the sky.

These clouds are more common in mountainous areas, but they are not as common in desert areas. They can only be spotted by a trained eye and are often a reflection of the surrounding sky.

When the air temperature falls, clouds form. In some places, these clouds are shaped like mountains, while others are flat and are formed over valleys. They also form over hills and are found at lower elevations. They come in a variety of sizes.

The most common types of clouds are called stratus clouds, while those at higher altitudes are called alto clouds. Stratus clouds are usually white or light gray and are not seen during the day.

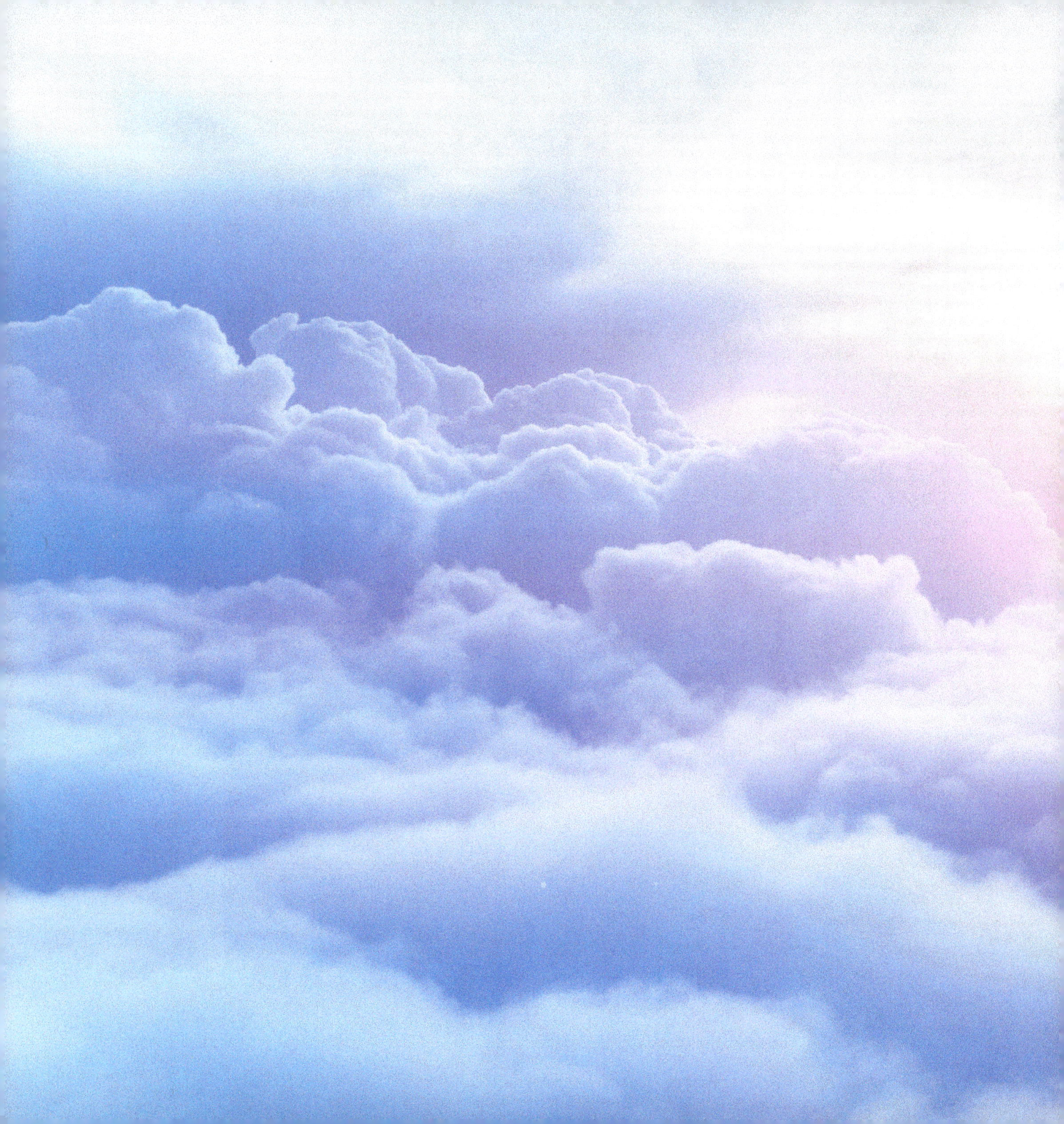

When it comes to the formation of clouds, it is important to know that they are made up of millions of very tiny drops of water and ice. While they look like giant, fluffy objects, they are actually the result of different atmospheric conditions.

This means that they are formed by different types of clouds. In addition to this, you can find out more about the different kinds of clouds and how they form in the sky. It is also helpful to know the names of some of the different kinds of cloud species.

The clouds are very interesting to watch. Even if they're not a real object, they can still make the sky look beautiful. This can be a useful tool in teaching your child about clouds and learning more about the world around them.

There are so many fun Facts About Clouds for kids that they will love. This can be a great way to engage your child in the natural world. There are many ways they can enjoy the beauty of the clouds.

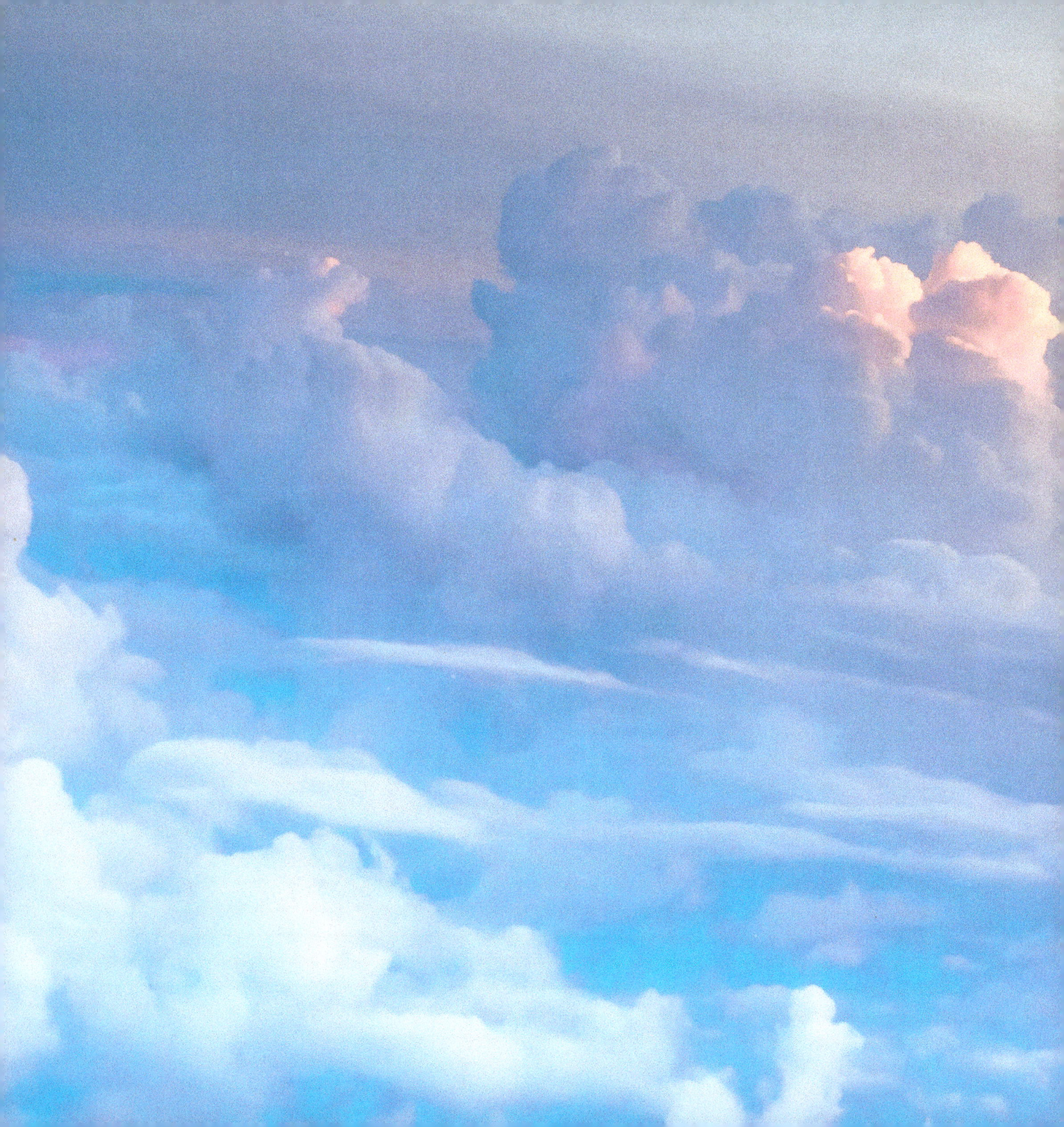

CPSIA information can be obtained
at www.ICGtesting.com
Printed in the USA
BVHW020219141122
651888BV00018B/532